Creating with
DRIFTWOOD
and
WEATHERED
WOOD

Innovations · Inspirations · Methods

Elyse and Mike Sommer

CROWN PUBLISHERS, INC., NEW YORK

Also by Elyse Sommer
THE BREAD DOUGH CRAFT BOOK
CONTEMPORARY COSTUME JEWELRY
DECOUPAGE: OLD AND NEW
DESIGNING WITH CUTOUTS
MAKE IT WITH BURLAP
ROCK AND STONE CRAFT

Inquiries should be addressed to Crown Publishers, Inc.
419 Park Avenue South, New York, N.Y. 10016

Library of Congress Catalog Card Number:
Printed in the United States of America
Published simultaneously in Canada by
General Publishing Company Limited
Design by Nedda Balter

CONTENTS

INTRODUCTION AND ACKNOWLEDGMENTS

The most exciting aspect of working with weathered wood is that the creative process begins the minute you select your raw material. When working in other media, the artist usually begins by going to his local arts and crafts supplier, armed with a list of recommended materials. When working with driftwood and weathered wood, he heads for the beach, lakeside, forest, desert, mountains, or open fields to pick and poke and search through the flotsam and jetsam tossed about by nature's forces. It is the artist's own vision that determines whether a piece of wood will remain abandoned or discarded or whether it will be rediscovered and reused. It is this need for making immediate and highly individualized choices about working materials that makes the medium so enormously appealing to anyone with a spirit of adventure and initiative, be he young or old, amateur or professional.

We have used both driftwood and weathered wood in our title though both words are basically interchangeable. Driftwood is wood floating on or cast ashore by the water. It becomes weathered by the action of the water and, once ashore, by the sun, wind, and rain. Most people associate driftwood with the fascinating gnarled shapes avidly collected and brought back from vacations at beaches. The driftwood artist is less dependent on the obviously beautiful and unusual pieces than the collector and may in fact be as turned on by ordinary planks, bits and pieces of smooth or rough wood, fall-offs from ships, and actual junk washed out to sea and back to shore again. At any rate, driftwood found along the shore is weathered wood.

Wood not found on or near water can also be weathered wood. An old barn or shed which has collapsed, old crates, doors and boxes, dried branches and tree stumps are all subject to the changes caused by the action of rain, sun, wind, and even fire.

All dried wood, no matter where it's found, is a natural plant material. The origin of the wood's plant family, the rocks and branches that might obstruct its growth, as well as the aforementioned weather factors all affect its shape and color. In picking up a piece of such wood, now nature's discard, and creating a new form, the weathered wood artist becomes intimately involved in the natural cycle. This is why wood evokes an emotional as well as an artistic response.

4

Just as the word "driftwood" has usually evoked visions of rare and unusually shaped pieces found at a beach, so driftwood art seems to have been identified chiefly with dried flower arrangements. In other words, driftwood, instead of being the star it deserves to be, has always been a mere prop. A piece of weathered wood can indeed be an integral part of a lovely floral arrangement or an assemblage of natural materials. However, the possibilities of weathered wood as an all-encompassing, independent art and craft are so vast that we consider our purpose here not just to inspire you with lots of ideas for creating beautiful art objects, but to take driftwood out of the "art prop" category once and for all.

Since art techniques have a way of transcending categories, there is a certain amount of overlapping throughout the book. Some of the work described in the chapter on Wood as a Canvas for paintings and some of the projects in the Flowers and Decorations chapter would be equally at home in the chapter on Sculpture and Construction.

Whether you attempt all or just some of the methods illustrated, everything you make will, by virtue of the uniqueness of each piece of wood, be completely original and one-of-a-kind. Your development as an artist is limited only by your energies in gathering your raw material, and your willingness to bring to your finds all the wit and imagination you have within you to give.

We would like to thank all the artists who so generously contributed their work to this book. Our special thanks to Jerry Holcomb, Sue Holcomb, Georgie Murphy, Milt Lev, and Lorena K. Sample who made it possible for us to be "armchair" collectors of California and Oregon driftwood as well as our own more readily available. East Coast wood. Our thanks also to Ben Ageman for his expert processing of our photographs.

All art work, unless otherwise credited, by Elyse Sommer.
All photographs, unless otherwise credited, by Mike Sommer.

A typical sight along a California or Oregon beach, driftwood piled along the beach so that you can literally walk on it. Photo courtesy Milt Lev.

Our own favorite hunting grounds, Silver Point at Atlantic Beach, Long Island. The beach comes to a point where ocean and bay converge and it is here that both the day's tide drifts and the things dumped by the cleanup tractors can be found.

Another view of Silver Point. A path, strewn with driftwood of all sorts, runs for about a mile alongside the rock jetties.

1 COLLECTING WOOD

In creating with driftwood, getting there is half the fun. Unlike the collector in search of the rare and perfect specimen, the artist-collector will be able to pick and choose from all sorts of interesting sites and never come home without some good finds.

Beaches are of course favorite driftwood hunting grounds. While there are plenty of beaches around the world, some are better than others, as anyone who has had the joy of literally walking on driftwood on a Maine island or along the coast of Oregon or California can tell you.

In places like these you will find many driftwood collectors. In our own New York areas driftwood is not quite as abundant, yet the diligent beach-comber can find plenty of workable materials. However, unless you're an early riser, you'll find many city- and town-maintained beaches cleaned up by tractor squads if you get there after ten o'clock in the morning. Private beaches and beach clubs often maintain a dumping area where the day's fresh driftwood along with scrap wood from beach shacks and cabanas is piled high to provide a veritable treasure trove for the astute picker. Some of the wood at a dump of this type may have been lying there for years, weathering to a lovely silver patina.

If you're a city dweller and don't have access to private town beaches or beach clubs, don't give up. You may not be able to do your collecting on a summer's day, cooling off with a swim afterwards, but you can usually drive right up to where the wood is any time other than the height of the summer vacation season, usually July Fourth to Labor Day. That leaves you with a pretty long season for collecting. There are also town and city dumps worth visiting.

Beachcombing can be as pleasant and as productive at the shores of either man-made or natural lakes, at the sides of streams or near riverbeds. While many people recommend late fall and winter as the best times to collect driftwood along the ocean, lake-combers suggest spring, before the lakes are full and right after the winter weather has bleached and cleansed the wood of silt and dirt. Streams and rivers often have inlets where wood piles up which can prove a bonanza for those hardy enough to climb along the sometimes rocky paths.

7

Weathered wooden lids from wire coil holders assembled into an 8½ by 10½ foot construction. Artist Warren Owens. Photographer Eric Pollitzer. Courtesy O. K. Harris Gallery, New York.

If you're particularly fond of the very bleached, silvery gray driftwood, don't neglect desert locales. Darker but equally beautifully grained woods may be found in mountain areas. Mountain-loving collectors consider July through September the best hunting season.

Finally, don't forget farm orchards and fields where you can find broken tree stumps, weathered barnwood, dried twigs and branches. Industrial dumps should not be overlooked either for unlikely but by no means unworkable types of weathered wood art sources. These might include the lids discarded from large wire coil spools which inspired Warren Owens to create an unusual construction called Frankie Fitz.

WHAT TO PICK

The pieces you select will depend not just on what's available on a particular day, but what you yourself are intent upon. The unusual collector's piece is something to be carried home as one would a trophy. Once cleaned, all it needs is a proper setting to show it off and enjoy.

If you're new to creating with driftwood and have no particular ideas in mind, you'll probably just walk along looking closely at what's on the ground, mentally trying to envision different forms and uses for what you see. The piece that sparks a response in you is the one you'll pick up. At first you might see only a random piece here and there that appeals to you, or in your first flush of excitement and enthusiasm you may pick up everything in sight until suddenly you can't carry any more. If you have a particular type of

An example of collector's quality driftwood used as a garden sculpture.

A stunning natural formation found at Ogonquit, Maine. Collection of Sol and Trudy Schwartz.

creation in mind, you may look for specific shapes, quickly skimming over and around those which you cannot use that day. One day you may be on the lookout for mostly curved sticks. Another day you may be particularly in need of flat boards and blocks. More often than not the pattern of your picking is determined by the distance you must carry your finds. Also, after a while you will find an amazing thing happening: pieces of wood will actually take on the shapes you are seeking. For example, if you're working on an animal sculpture, many of the pieces you pick up will look like animals to you; yet, if on another day you are looking for potential faces to make something like the assemblage on page 00, the same animal shapes will now suggest human heads. And so it goes. When you create with driftwood and weathered wood, selection *is* creation!

ALWAYS USEFUL PIECES

While some of the wood you gather may never live up to its original promise in terms of developing into a work of art, there are certain commonly found shapes which are always useful. As you begin to work with driftwood you should at all times have at hand at least a fair assortment of straight and curved sticks, boards, planks, and flat-bottomed wood chunks in various sizes. If nothing else, the planks and chunks can always be used as props or mountings for all types of art work.

Unlike more conventional art media where overbuying and oversupplying can constitute costly mistakes, you can't really make any mistakes in collecting driftwood—as a very last resort, there's always the fireplace.

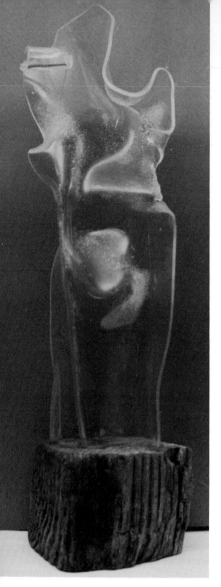

A weathered tree stump serves as a perfect prop for a large stone. The stone is glued to the wood with lots of white glue.

A driftwood block makes a fine foundation for an abstract plexiglass sculpture. Mike Sommer.

TIPS FOR SAFE AND SENSIBLE COLLECTING

1. Carry a heavy canvas bag which can be slung over your shoulder. This will enable you to carry home a maximum supply with a minimum of stress on your arms and back.
2. Don't try to carry too much. If you want a very heavy piece, be sure to get someone to help you. Sprained backs and stomach muscles do nothing to spur on the creative muse.
3. Carry a small saw and a hammer so that you can cut small pieces from larger ones you don't need.
4. When walking along jetties, in woods, along wood- and rock-strewn beaches, wear comfortable and sturdy-soled shoes.
5. Wear a hat when collecting on a hot sunny day.
6. Pick a long stick and use it as a poker before picking pieces out of a pile of rubble. Sometimes there's a lot of tar in a pile of wood and the poking stick will avoid your getting it onto your hands.
7. For extensive collecting trips, take along a sandwich and an apple. Bending and lifting combined with fresh air create a mighty appetite.
8. If driving to a beach where cars are allowed to ride along the sand, don't do it unless you are experienced at this type of driving. Cars get stuck in sand quite easily unless a driver knows exactly what to do, so the average reader would be well advised to park near the beach but not on it and do some extra walking and lugging.

2 WORKING TECHNIQUES AND TOOLS

Weathered wood art is inexpensive and simple, not only because the raw material is free and plentiful but because very few tools are required. Some artists are purists about touching the wood in terms of altering the shape, the color, or even polishing the surface. Those who do alter the basic wood to conform to a particular design plan usually strive to maintain the feeling and patina of the wood. Our own feeling about driftwood techniques is that the artist's own vision should be the determining factor. The examples shown in this book are predominantly "natural," but not exclusively so. The various painted, cut, carved, and sawed pieces easily hold their own with the others. Thus, whatever methods are employed to make your creation are the right methods to use in that particular instance.

DRYING AND WEATHERING

Unless wood has been lying on dry ground for a long time, it usually needs to be cured. In many instances this is the only thing you have to do before working with the wood. Let the wood dry very slowly to avoid cracking. It's best to spread it out to permit air circulation and prevent any mildew from forming. If you live in a house with a boiler room, which is usually warm and dry, spread some newspapers on the floor and lay out the pieces. During summer months, when a boiler is not in full operation, small, very wet pieces can be placed on the flat top of the boiler itself. If you live in an apartment, spread the wood out on the bottom of a large carton and turn it often so that the air gets to all parts of the wood. During dry weather, the wood can be spread on a table on a porch or in a yard. The longer you let the wood dry, the more permanently cured it will be.

Driftwood found after it has been lying on the ground for a long time usually has a natural silvery or pale beige patina which is greatly treasured. Freshly washed ashore wood can be given the weathered patina simply by exposing it further to the elements. Contrary to what many people believe, you don't have to live near salt water to be able to weather wood in this way. We've often left wood out on a picnic table in our yard which is five miles from a beach and seen it weathering in just a week of being exposed to ordinary sun, wind, and rain.

Artist Ahuvah Bebe Dushey has set aside this whole area at the side of her house on Long Island's South Shore as a bleaching yard for the wood she collects.

The bleaching process can be hurried and intensified by soaking wood in a solution of half household bleach and half water. The wood can also be brushed with undiluted bleach for a yellow-brown finish, or treated with wood bleach for a plaster-white surface.

CLEANING

Wood that is covered with silt or other clinging soil should be washed, using a hard (wire brushes are excellent) brush to scrub the surface. Some people wash all their found wood in water and detergent but this is a matter of personal choice.

Bark and pitch embedded in the wood itself is like a layer of extra skin and should be scraped or sanded away. This is done most easily while the wood is wet.

TOOLS

A few simple hand tools are really the only musts for weathered wood-crafting:

A small awl and/or an X-Acto knife can be used to do any cleaning and picking jobs. If you buy an X-Acto knife with router blade attachments (#5 X-Acto) you will have a tool suitable for carving as well as any kind of cleaning and picking jobs (though for large carved sculptures you would need heavier chisels. See Chapter 7).

X-Acto #5 knife is suitable for any kind of wood cleaning or picking, as well as light carving. Photo courtesy X-Acto, Inc.

A variety of replacement blades are available with the X-Acto knife. Photo courtesy X-Acto, Inc.

For joining of wood you will need hammer, nails, and/or wood dowels. Wood can also be glued with white resin glues. For glued wood that will be kept outdoors, epoxy cement is recommended. Epoxy resin can be used as a weatherproof finish.

A coping saw is necessary to saw and cut.

Garnet paper or a small rasp can be used for sanding and contouring.

All the above are hardware store items, and if you have any sort of tool chest you probably own all of them already. If you do a lot of sculpturing and sawing, you can, of course, simplify your work tremendously by using electric tools. Some of the illustrations in the book show power tools rather than hand tools in use. However, this is a matter of convenience and preference. Everything can be fashioned with the above-mentioned hand tools.

Illustrated here are some of the tools, both hand and power types, which we have found most useful for weathered wood crafting.

Some of the tools you might use to cut, contour, and sand wood. At the front a coping saw and next to it a rasp. These basic tools could suffice. Electric jigsaws are useful if you plan a lot of wood sawing. The Dremel Moto Shop is a small but very complete workshop complete with jigsaw, sanding discs, as well as an attachment for routing and drilling.

An awl is handy for picking dirt out of wood crevices and to mark wood for drilling. An electric drill, while not a necessity, is handy since it will also have attachments for routing (shown in photo) and sanding.

A sanding disc with tiny flexible abrasive wheels which may be attached to any electric drill is an excellent tool for cleaning and polishing wood. Photo courtesy Merit Abrasive Products, Inc.

The Sando-Flex abrasive wheel can also be used to contour sand wood as shown. Photo courtesy Merit Abrasive Products, Inc.

POLISHING

One of the simplest and most natural polishing methods is that by which the wood is rubbed with the tip of a deer's horn. Deer-horn polishing compresses the wood fibers and creates a soft sheen. Some artists polish only areas they want to highlight. Deer horns are popular with jewelry makers and you may find them in jewelry and bead supply stores. (See Sources of Supplies.)

In addition to or instead of deer-horn-tip polishing you can rub your finished work with wax. We have spoken to people who have used everything from shoe polish to floor polish and car Simoniz. There are some polishes designed especially for driftwood (see Sources of Supplies). Whatever wax you use, the procedure is always to rub the polish into the wood with your hand since the hand warmth creates a soft effect. This is also known as French polishing. A toothbrush can be used for getting wax into crevices. Buff with a soft cloth or a clean brush.

Wood being polished with a deerhorn tip. Wax can be used in addition to or instead of the deerhorn.

COLORING WOOD

Although most driftwood artists seem to prefer the natural look, wood can be interesting and attractive with the help of a variety of coloring materials. You can use artist's oils, acrylic or plastic paints, household types of latex paints, or a variety of stains to color your wood. A good method of achieving color without losing the grain is to apply a transparent stain of artist's oils thinned with turpentine, watercolor, or acrylic paints thinned by one-half with water. Matte or gloss media may be brushed over stained or unstained wood to seal the surface. Decorative methods and techniques will be discussed as they are applied to specific projects.

Many of the old wagons still in use in Italy have weathered wood sides elaborately painted with colorful scenes. Discarded wagon boards are treasured by collectors. ➜ Italian wagon board painted with scenes from *Cavalleria Rusticana* on each panel. Collection of Vera and Bernard Lippe.

3 WOOD AS A CANVAS

The texture and irregularity of weathered wood make it an ideal natural canvas for a variety of art techniques. The wood requires no priming. Most painters prefer acrylics rather than oils since wood is highly absorbent and acrylics tend to take hold better. Whichever type of paint is used, it is usually best to use paints more sparingly on wood than on conventional canvases in order to maintain the natural and untouched feeling.

If a wood surface is fairly smooth, designs may be applied with India ink. Crow quill pens are available in all art supply stores and you can try them out in a range of replaceable points. We like the flexible crow quill point.

Magic markers also work very well on wood. Be sure to use those which are marked PERMANENT AND WATERPROOF. Even coloring pencils can be used. Well-sharpened oil color pencils such as Derwent or Eagle Prismatic work very well. The colors can be superimposed on one another and blended with a lighter shade so that they will have a water-color rather than a crayoned look. This technique might have special appeal for those who feel timid about painting. In fact, designs can actually be traced onto the wood, like needle-point designs, using a dark pencil to outline and then coloring in.

The cut paper techniques of the collage artists and decoupeurs may also be applied to wood. The highly varnished finish of conventional decoupage can be used, but I find that pasting down the design with a matte medium varnish and glazing it with two or three coats of the same medium (omitting the traditional varnishing-sanding-waxing procedures) is more compatible with weathered wood.

A lovely drawing in permanent brown magic marker on a weathered wood shingle. Dee Weber.

An impressively large and weatherbeaten oval board makes a fine background for another decoupage scene. The wood was mottled to a yellowish green tint which blended with the grasses and serves as a perfect background for the Audubon birds. Eleanor Hasbrouck Rawlings.

Seascapes have great affinity with driftwood. This one is done with hand-colored decoupage designs. The uneven, jagged edges of the wood are used to suggest water.

The intricate details of this ship were drawn on pale gray weathered wood in India ink. Joseph Honings.

Just enough acrylic paint is used to bring out the owl in a weathered log. C. Bert Webber, artist and photographer.

17

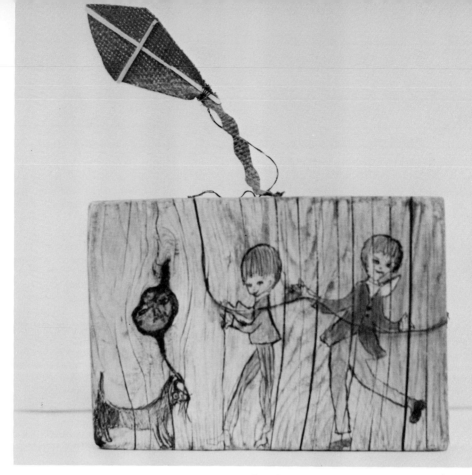

Colored crayon drawing on a block of silver gray wood. The design grew out of the natural whorl in the wood which somehow suggested a sun-shaped kite. The children's kite is glue-stiffened burlap with crossbars fashioned from toothpicks. The wire cord is nailed down at the top and so that it fits into the children's hands. There are two more children at either end of the block. (See color section.)

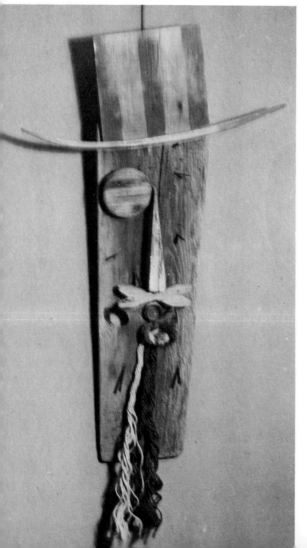

Red, white, and blue acrylics are used for a delightful weathered wood Uncle Sam. Mabel D'Amico, artist. Photographed at the Firehouse Gallery, Nassau Community College. (See color section.)

DECOULLAGE OR THREE-DIMENSIONAL DECOUPAGE-COLLAGE

The combination of precisely cut paper designs (decoupage) plus torn papers (collage) can be further enhanced with such three-dimensional effects as raised rather than cut letters; stone, wood, or shell heads added to a flat body. The word découllage (pronounce it day-coo-lahj) seems a good name for this combination of methods.

A striking ad for a man's suit in which the model's head was actually missing brought to mind the title "Armchair Politician." The paper was sprayed twice on each side with clear plastic spray to give it more body for cutting and pasting down. Orange art tissue, torn to loosely conform to the outline of the wood, was used to seal and color the deeply grained wood. After the cut figure was pasted in place with acrylic matte medium, blue paint thinned to a watery consistency was brushed into the wood and over the art tissue. A head of driftwood was glued in place. The armchair politician's newspaper was adhered to cardboard, brushed several times with the medium, and when dry, nailed in place. (See color section.)

Another fashion ad triggered this découllage idea. Torn blue tissue was used as a background and pebbles selected in a variety of skin tones were glued over the heads in the cutout design. Plastic letters serve as a platform for the figures and to spell out the title which is an inherent part of the design.

SAND PAINTING AND COLLAGE

Sometimes the least likely pieces of wood result in the most interesting ideas. Beaches and wood dumps abound with very thin, irregular boards, with edges that seem to be almost peeling or unraveling. The shapes, more than the texture or color of these pieces, seem to suggest all sorts of possibilities. By covering the surface with a mixture of sand and glue, it is possible to create fascinating sand paintings and collages.

Glue diluted by one-third with water is brushed over the surface of wood.

Sand is sprinkled into the wet glue. Any sand which does not adhere can be shaken off. Any areas not covered can be brushed with more glue, with a bit more sand sprinkled in place.

Acrylics thinned with water are used to create a sand painting inspired by traditional Indian designs. The outline may be drawn first using India ink and a crow quill pen. Be sure to keep wiping your pen point with a rag before dipping into ink since it will pick up some of the sand.

An abstract collage on a sanded finish. Both the twig bodies and the shell heads are adhered with five-minute epoxy.

BEACH SCENES ON SANDED WOOD

The sanded wood finish seems to have unlimited possibilities. A beach scene which seems a "natural" provides an opportunity to bring a wealth of different materials together. Planks of weathered wood make fine houses. Use fairly thin planks, no thicker than ¼ inch and save the edges for your eaves. The raw edges can be stained with a bit of thinned paint. Twigs can be rasped flat and used to suggest house steps. Bits of floral moss and dried flowers can be used as gardens, and dried weeds add the flavor of wild dunes or just contrast. Realistic touches such as sea gulls can be painted in, or created with modeling paste, cut blow-fish bones, or found hidden in the centers of large sand dollars abundant at the western Florida beaches.

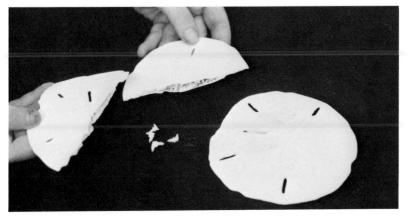

If you find any of these large sand dollars, break them in half gently and you will find little white doves inside.

Beach scene on sanded wood. (See color section for another of these collages.)

Materials used to create the beach scene: House shape cut from thin driftwood board, edges of the wood for eaves, twigs sanded flat for steps (for more detailed driftwood houses see Chapter 5, page 42). To make small gardens, dried flowers are stuck into the top of small squares of Styrofoam and covered with floral moss. Floral clay which is available in large rolls as shown at the top, is used to attach the moss to the Styrofoam and the Styrofoam to the background.

WOODBURNT DESIGNS OR PYROGRAPHY

The woodburning pencil is an easy-to-use, inexpensive tool, long popular for camp and scout projects but somehow first beginning to be discovered as a tool source for more sophisticated crafts work. The pencil can be plugged into any electric outlet and heats up almost instantly. It takes little time or effort to learn the variations of strokes possible. Broad strokes can be made by applying pressure to the side of the pencil, and working it very slowly. Fine lines such as facial features are achieved with quick, light strokes of the pencil tip. The pencil is actually burning or etching a design into the wood.

Every one of the faces in the old printer's typecase shown here was burnt in with a woodburning pencil. The designs can be burnt directly into the wood, or you can use an ordinary India ink pen to lightly draw in the areas where eyes, mouth, and nose will go. An interesting aspect of this particular demonstration project is that it illustrates how many uses there are for many of the plain, apparently dull and ordinary little pieces of driftwood so often passed by. Some were cut to fit the boxes and to emphasize "necks" but most were used as they were found. Velverette, a thick white crafts glue, was used to adhere the wood to the background.

Some wood shapes which lend themselves to woodburning faces.

An India ink pen can be used to mark off features as a guide for the woodburning pencil.

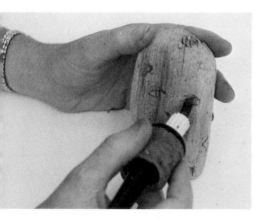

The point of the woodburning pencil is used to etch the features into the wood.

All kinds of woodburnt faces glued into an old printer's typecase. The title is woodburnt onto a block of wood cut to fit one of the boxes.

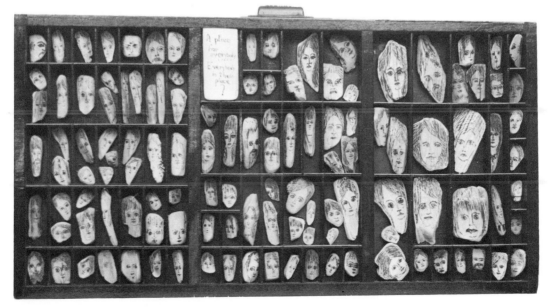

Woodburnt portraits can be done on a larger and more elaborate scale. Very smooth weathered wood, or wood which has been sanded smooth, can be stained with oil or thinned acrylic paints. The effect of the colors adhering to the etched details is very striking and rich. (See color section.)

A woodburnt portrait on a larger scale. Standing wood forms like this can be used functionally as bookends, or the top area of the head could be routed or carved out to accommodate dried flowers and weeds.

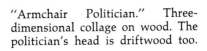

"Armchair Politician." Three-dimensional collage on wood. The politician's head is driftwood too.

Driftwood pendants with ivory, coral, and shell inlays. The green pendant is stained with green and gold coloring pencils.

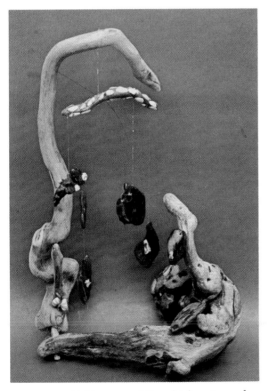

Tabletop mobile which gains color from its reddish wood components, tiny pastel shells, and bits of coral glued to some of the mobile pieces.

Carved sea horn weed holder.

Driftwood assemblage set in plaster. Mike Sommer.

Driftwood used as the loom for weaving. Mary Mendoza.

Real ostrich egg cut out with electric cutting tool, mounted on red cypress. The interior scene features fairy driftwood with shell flowers. Julia Hernberg, artist. George Schupka, photographer.

"Uncle Sam." Acrylics and colored rope on driftwood. Mabel D'Amico. Photo courtesy of the artist.

"At the Beach." Collage on wood covered with glue and sand.

"Go Fly a Kite." Colored crayons used to draw design on wood. The dog's kite is a natural whorl in the wood.

Assemblage of crafts and collectibles in weathered drawer. The print is framed with driftwood sticks; the stone figure and decoupaged egg are mounted on driftwood.

Driftwood incorporated into weaving. Mary Mendoza.

Color-stained carving.
Collection of the authors.

∪-shaped fence, part of an entire alphabet series created by A. William Clark. Photo courtesy of the artist.

Jerry Holcomb mounts some of her choicest pieces of polished driftwood on velvet to make a free-form collage. Photo courtesy of the artist.

"Treasure Box." Tiny gold box is covered with gold cloth, lined with mirrors, edged with gold beads. The mirrors reflect what seem to be dancers of tiny driftwood formations with mother of pearl "heads." Mabel D'Amico. Photo courtesy of the artist.

Decoullage, a word coined to describe this combination of decoupage and collage techniques: decoupage cut figures, torn art tissue, pebbles, and plastic letters.

"The Egghead." A woven wood construction.

Woodburnt portrait on sanded and stained weathered board. Thinned oil colors are rubbed into the etched design. Collection of the authors.

4 WOOD ASSEMBLAGES AND WALL RELIEFS

Weathered wood is a very versatile wall relief medium. The wood can be used as a base on which to create projecting designs, or the designs themselves can be made with wood, or wood plus other materials. You have already seen an example of assemblage in the woodburnt faces demonstrated in the last chapter. Now let's explore assemblages and reliefs in some other variations.

ASSEMBLING BEACH FINDS AND OTHER COLLECTIBLES ON WOOD

One of the easiest and most popular forms of assemblage is to make an artistic arrangement on a well-weathered, interestingly shaped board. The wood should be compatible with the mounted objects in both shape and texture. The examples shown here were not mounted as found. In fact, the shells and bits of beach glass were picked specifically to go with the ship-shaped wood and the faces were inked in to carry out the idea of different types of people, all at sea.

A collection of more rare and perfect (in the collector's sense, that is) shells could be assembled with nothing added but glue. Dried flowers, weeds, and pods are other good materials for beginning efforts in assemblage. Light materials can be mounted with white glue. Shells, stones, glass, and other heavier objects are best adhered with five-minute epoxy.

To make an assemblage of inked shell faces, collect a variety of shell shapes and colors. Bits of beach glass and pebbles can be worked in also. Turn the shells in different ways, contour or convex sides facing up, in order to "see" a variety of faces. Even broken shells work out well.

Features can be drawn directly onto shells which require no preparation other than washing and drying. A flexible crow quill pen with a point most comfortable for you works best. Shown here is a flexible crow quill pen.

A variety of shell faces mounted on a silvery, ship-shaped piece of wood. The semibald man at the top center is drawn on green beach glass. Note how the shells are mounted at random.

These genuine arrowheads dating from 3500 B.C. to A.D. 1000 were sent by a friend from Texas. They are indeed collector's items and seemed to call for Indian type faces to emphasize their shape, texture, and historic significance.

RELIEF SCULPTURES ON WOOD

Barbara Moscow works with a variety of self-hardening sculpturing materials such as Instant Machie and Sculptamold. She looks for odd shapes of weathered wood and plans her relief sculpture to conform to the background contours. Often she incorporates pieces of wood into the relief design. For the beginner she recommends that a sketch be made first. This can be drawn directly onto the wood. Both Instant Machie and Sculptamold are mixed with water. The Sculptamold, which is a plaster material, dries to a smooth white finish, the papier-mâché, to a gray, stonelike finish. The latter is somewhat easier to use since it takes longer to set. With Sculptamold you have to work a bit faster since it dries rock hard within half an hour. Be sure to have a damp rag at hand to clean up any excess bits of the clay as you go along. (See Sources of Supplies for Sculptamold and Instant Machie.)

The relief on these two doors was designed so that each piece could stand independently if desired. Barbara Moscow.

ASSEMBLAGE ON A LARGE SCALE

The true potential of weathered wood is perhaps best expressed by those artists who work on a large scale. A wall executed by A. William Clark for the assembly hall of the student center at the State University at Albany is a stunning example of weathered wood assemblage. The artist worked around a basic tripartite design plan and compiled the components of the wall from his own treasure trove of "junk," gifts from everyone who followed the project (which had to be completed in seven days), and materials gathered at the city dump. After the base wall had been covered with plywood, the artist, with the help of some students, applied all the pieces of his assemblage with nails and white glue. The door and the e. e. cummings poem were used to divide the tripartite sections. The finished wall was partially sprayed with off-white latex paint and the bottom was dry-brushed with the same paint. The way all the diverse elements, both the wood and the unusual additions such as the old television set, mesh so perfectly reflects the artist's earlier interest and training in mosaic making. A similar wall was scaled down to fit the artist's own living room, and his kitchen is completely panelled in weathered wood.

Wall of weathered wood plus found objects from Assembly Hall of the Student Center at the State University of New York at Albany. A. William Clark. Photo courtesy of the artist.

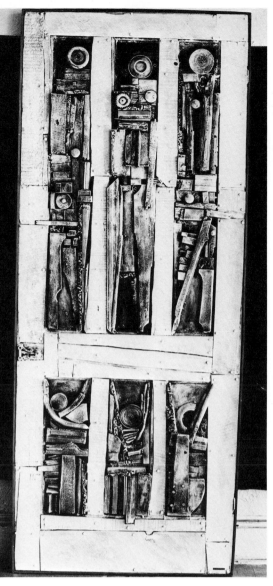

"4½ Figures." A. William Clark. Scraps of wood and old toys are inserted into the panels of a door and framed with pine from the back of old pictures. The inserts were painted black and dry-brushed with white. The pine is slightly dry-brushed in white. Photo courtesy of the artist.

Weathered wood boxes, nailed together and filled with a variety of weathered found wood items, including some old wooden bowls. Ahuvah Bebe Dushey.

"Avalon Cindy" was made by A. William Clark during a week at Avalon, New Jersey. A four-foot round of plywood was covered with white glue, weathered wood, and a variety of miscellany. Sand and pebbles were used to fill in some of the spaces and the entire composition covered with polyester resin. Photo courtesy of the artist.

BOXED ASSEMBLAGES

Many artists have been fascinated with the assemblage possibilities of wooden boxes. The late Joseph Cornell was noted for his ingenious boxes, which he filled with an array of charming nostalgia. Whether large or small, rough and unfinished or not, boxes do indeed lend themselves to an amazing variety of assemblage compositions. Sometimes you can find boxes all ready for assemblage. An old toolbox or shelf drawer, abandoned amid a pile of wood junk, assumes a casual elegance once weathered. In addition to the boxes themselves, there are box lids for slimmer constructions. Since wood is very light in weight you can extend your use of boxes to include frames since the lighter weight wood pieces can be glued into open frames as well as boxes with backboards.

An old box filled with driftwood, some carved wood discards, and gracefully framed with wood from an old knife holder which was allowed to fall apart and weather. Ahuvah Bebe Dushey, artist. Photo, Glenn Usdin.

The interesting holes in this wood were the result of termite erosion. When a friend brought these "treasures" to Ahuvah Bebe Dushey, she glued them together with some other found wood into an old weathered box. Photo Glenn Usdin.

An old tool drawer becomes a charming assemblage of handmade and antique objects. A handcolored print is framed with weathered wood sticks; a tiny stone sculpture rests on a bit of driftwood, as does the decoupaged egg box in the lower left corner. (See color section.)

CIGAR BOX FRAMES

For small assemblages, you'll find wooden cigar boxes very versatile. Shown here are single-box assemblages. Larger units can be assembled by nailing a series of boxes together.

A few pieces of polished and carved wood plus a cookie cutter offer textural contrast to driftwood and a piece of cork mounted into a wooden cigar box.

You can actually use your boxes in a utilitarian way. Here is a cigar box jewelry box, with a lid design of polished driftwood pieces. The little doglike piece of wood at the front of the lid has a nail punched through it and thus serves as a decorative closing knob.

Styrofoam, cut to fit the inside dimensions of the box, is glued in place. A mirror is glued to the center and a random design of driftwood worked all around. The Styrofoam makes both vertical and horizontal placements possible. Some of the longer pieces are pushed into the Styrofoam. The mirror should be kept covered with masking tape until all the gluing is complete.

PLASTER AND WOOD ASSEMBLAGE
IN A HANDMADE BOX

A box to custom fit a particular design plan can be easily assembled from strips of pine and a Masonite backing. A relief incorporating many fragments of driftwood plus other found objects is first arranged into a ½-inch-thick piece of Styrofoam cut to fit the inside of the frame. This makes it possible to assemble the entire composition, study it, and make changes and adjustments before affixing it permanently inside the frame. Once the design is set up, plaster is poured into the frame and the entire design, still set into the Styrofoam arranging base, is slipped into the plaster. The finished work can be hung or displayed as a tabletop sculpture, giving you two distinctly different views.

The demonstration that follows was created and photographed by Mike Sommer.

Box frame constructed from pine strips and Masonite backing. The inside edges are taped to prevent plaster from oozing. Three holes are drilled in each side so that nails (or dowels) can be pushed into the cement to permanently bind the set cement and the frame together.

The design is set into Styrofoam so that an overall perspective of the composition can be studied at leisure. Since the Styrofoam used is only ¼-inch thick a supporting wooden board is kept underneath.

Cement is poured slowly. It will be poured up to the holes which will allow space for displacement resulting from the setting in of the design.

The design, *with* the Styrofoam base intact, is gently slid off the wooden base and into the cement.

The design in the box, the nails are pushed in place.

The finished assemblage in hanging position. (See color section.)

5 SCULPTURE AND CONSTRUCTION

Since assemblage is a three-dimensional method, this chapter is actually a continuation and extension of the last.

NATURAL SCULPTURES

In every driftwood artist's path there are bound to fall some natural configurations which require absolutely nothing but the moment of recognition for the sculpture to be complete. The illustration on page 9 in Chapter 1 is an impressive example of such a natural sculpture. Shown here is an equally exciting smaller natural sculpture which required only a base for mounting to be complete. Yet, even with a sculpture so self-sufficient, the artistic thought process can at times continue so that with only a slight addition of another element, a different sort of statement can be made. In this case, the addition of a pebble turned what seemed destined to be some type of prehistoric ani-

A lovely natural sculpture suggests some sort of strange prehistoric beast, mounted on a piece of driftwood by means of drilling and gluing.

The natural sculpture is given a new artistic interpretation with the addition of a single pebble.

mal and nothing else, into a different sort of creature, raising a philosophic question about "Man and Beast." To mount sculptures of this type, drill or rout out holes deep enough for the sculpture to rest securely. Pour white glue into the grooves and set in the wood. Let the piece either lie or rest against a wall so that no pressure is applied until the glue is completely set.

LENDING NATURE A HELPING HAND

Sometimes a piece of driftwood seems to ask for a certain form, but some alterations or additions are required to bring that particular image to life. Some artists have a sort of religious fanaticism about being true to the basic material and consider any tampering with the shape a breach of artistic integrity. Anyone who feels like this will have to wait to make a dancing figure sculpture until nature provides one complete with arms and legs. The sculptor with a bent for a bit of surgery can add that which he sees in his mind but which nature has forgotten to provide, or possibly destroyed.

The back of the dancing figure showing the arms, rasped down to fit into the small of the back and nailed in place. The lower leg was added the same way.

37

Dancing figures complete with arms and two legs are rarely found. The arms and part of one leg were added. The head is a quail's egg, stuffed with Instant Machie and painted tan. The steps were found as seen and are actually fairly common configurations. Steps of any height could be constructed from different sized blocks of wood.

FANCIFUL SCULPTURES

Driftwood formations often bring out an artist's sense of humor. Shown here are some examples.

Mary Mendoza introduces movement into this sculpture which actually seesaws.

A lovable sort of chap to bring a smile to anyone's face. Mary Mendoza.

From the moment this wood with its long narrow recess was sighted it suggested a bus. The bus driver and passengers are made from shells and stones. The wheels are painted drawer knobs and the letters are from an old print set. The window separations are small twigs.

This whale-shaped wood was fortuitously cracked so that tiny white shell teeth could be glued in place for a more realistic effect. The stand was a piece of found wood with a handy back ledge.

Driftwood can be used as humorous commentary on the happenings in the world. The base for this somber-looking politician was painted green and white with raised plastic letters, an exact replica of road signs around the nation's capital.

Artist Mary Prisco collected a whole menagerie of animals and mounted them on a cart made from pieces of boxes and other bits of wood. Photo courtesy *Good Housekeeping,* photograph Ernest Silva.

So many small pieces of wood seem to look like owls. Here's a whole owl tree. Touches of ink are used to accent feathers, eyes, and beaks.

CONSTRUCTIONS

Many times individual pieces of wood, while lovely, gain importance and purpose when built into a larger construction. Other pieces which have neither meaning nor beauty when isolated, can be constructed into highly original and distinctive sculptural units.

Large pieces of driftwood nailed together into a sectional fence. Each of the three parts of the fence could be used individually. The one large rectangular piece was an old headboard put out to bleach. The ladderlike piece was once part of a boat. Ahuvah Bebe Dushey. Photograph, Ron Feigenbaum.

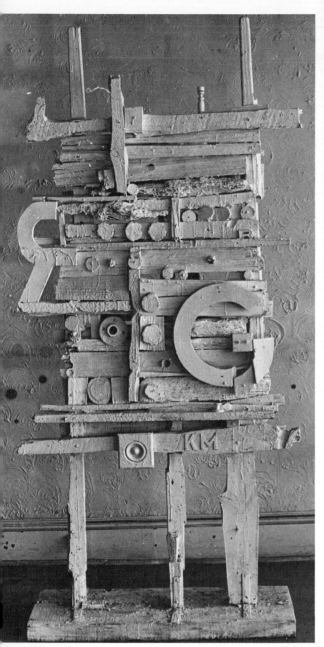

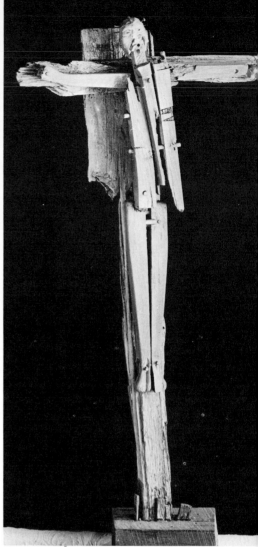

Crucifixion by A. William Clark. The head was salvaged from an old plaster statue. Photo courtesy author.

"Vexillary Figure" by A. William Clark. Found wood plus letters from a sign screwed together and painted with white latex. Photo courtesy artist.

REALISTIC CONSTRUCTIONS

The driftwood beach house, featured as part of the sand collage in Chapter 1, was just an abstract of a house, lacking windows or other realistic details. If you'd like to reproduce a particular house in driftwood, you will be interested in the way Robert Gofonia constructs his authentic driftwood replicas. The artist first became interested in this craft while working with the New York State Hudson River Valley Commission. He took part in the preparation of a report regarding the preservation of lighthouses in the Hudson River, and the beauty of these lighthouses moved him to a desire to re-create them in a unique manner. The medium he chose was aged driftwood from the river itself. Upon moving to Long Island he was once again inspired to reconstruct historic buildings. In the following pages he shares with us his procedures in constructing one of his houses. Photographs are by William T. Higgins and Ron Orcutt.

A photograph of the structure to be reproduced is translated into a rough sketch, then a construction paper cutout. From this cutout a template is made out of Masonite, which will be a back-up for the final plaque.

The parts of the structure are glued, one piece at a time, to the template.

Small strips of well-weathered wood (usually edges of old baskets) are cut for window, roof, and door trims and for laminating the sides of the main body.

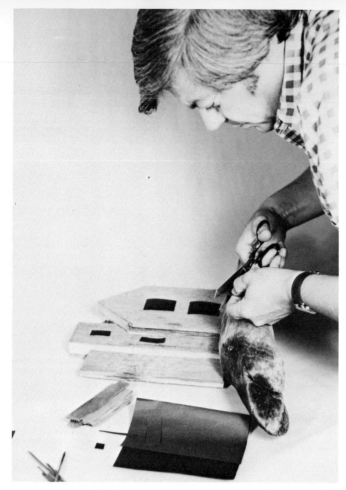

Black construction paper is used for window back-up.

The windows are trimmed with the weathered strips.

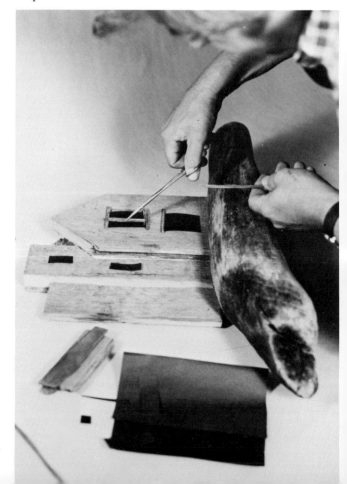

Here is the finished house, complete with roofs and chimney.

Another charming reproduction of an old Long Island house.

Old Long Island house in driftwood.

Another simple and charming house. Note the way a piece of driftwood is used to create the front entry overhang.

6 MOBILES

When Alexander Calder created his first light moveable constructions in the late 1920s he truly brought sculpture into the twentieth century. The French artist Duchamp applied the name "mobile" to Calder's creations and the word has been synonymous ever since with all works of art depending on movement of any kind for their appeal. The popularity of mobiles is evidenced by the mobiles hanging not just in museums, but in shopwindows, commercial building lobbies, schools, and homes. Amateur as well as professional craftsmen in every medium have been fascinated with the technique of mobile making, and the driftwood artist is no exception.

To make a mobile you will need assorted pieces of driftwood, nylon fishing line for connecting the pieces, and a brass hook for hanging the completed mobile. The only tool you will need is a small drill bit in either a hand or electric drill to make stringing holes in your driftwood. Milt Lev, an avid driftwood mobile maker, demonstrates in the following pages how he makes a mobile.

Designing, as with all driftwood art, begins with one's choice of materials.

Here is the artist lugging home a plentiful supply to give himself lots of "play" as he plans his mobiles.

Pieces of driftwood are laid out on a table in the desired configuration. Plan the design to avoid collision when the mobile is in motion.

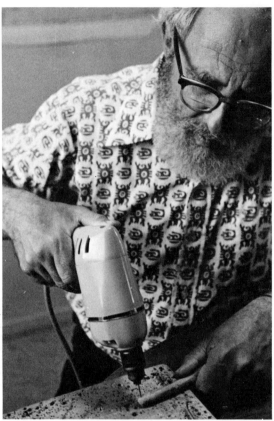

Holes are drilled at the connecting points. It is best to first mark the hole to be drilled with an awl.

Each piece for the mobile is polished with a deerhorn tip. Outdoor mobiles should be left unpolished.

Don't skimp on the length of fishing line you use for stringing your mobile components. It is very frustrating to tie extremely short ends.

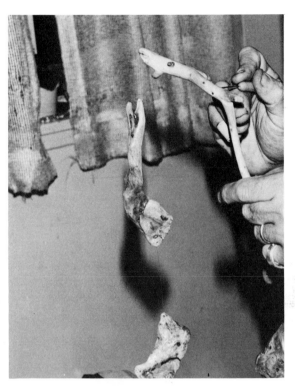

A needle is used to try to locate the correct point of balance. The pictured attempt is unsuccessful.

Successful location of balance point.

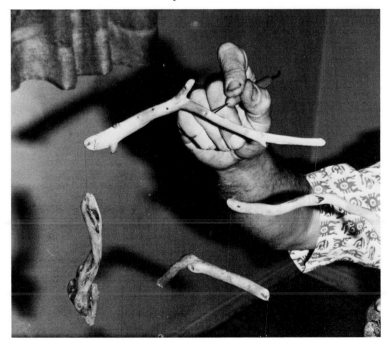

The finished mobile.

A larger mobile with many unusual shapes.

Mobile combining wood with shells.

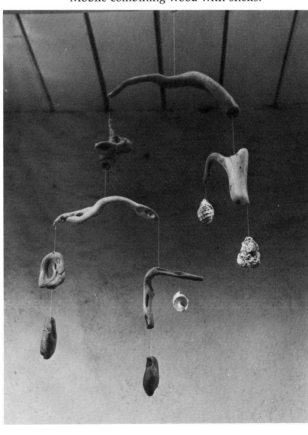

Photos of the artist at the beach by Marge Lev; photos of the mobile-in-the-making by Loli Sergo; photos of the finished mobiles by the artist.

DRIFTWOOD AND GLASS FLOAT MOBILES

Glass floats, lost overboard mainly from Japanese fishing boats, have become among the most coveted collectors' items of beachcombers along the Oregon coast. Rumor has it that these floats, which can range in size from small to giant-sized balls weighing as much as forty or more pounds, are made from old Coke bottles. Since genuine glass floats (as floats have increased in value and popularity, imitations have flourished) usually have blue-green hues, this may well be true. Whatever their source, these floats are well worth the search, along with all kinds of other unbroken bottles and even light bulbs. What with the buffeting of the winds and the obstruction of reefs, any of these floats found intact are not just lovely to own, but seem a true miracle of nature. These glass gems are obviously rarer than drift-wood, but when they're found it is right amidst the driftwood piled up along the coastline. Naturally, a beachcomber lucky enough to find some floats will want to display them in an appropriate setting. One of the most attractive ways of showing off a glass float is to make it a part of a mobile. The concept of the glass and driftwood combined can be adapted to attractive bottles which might be more accessible to the average driftwood mobile maker.

It takes an alert beachcomber to spot a glass float among a pile of driftwood (see float within the marked circle). Photo © Bert Webber.

A prize-winning mobile of driftwood, glass floats, and seaweed. The seaweed was found in this shape and condition on the beach near Oregon's Winchuck River. Photo © Bert Webber, artist-photographer.

TABLETOP MOBILES

Mobiles can also be suspended from bases which sit on a table, or if very large, on the floor. For a table model, you can attach a curved piece of driftwood to your base either with a dowel or nails. If you don't have a driftwood suspension bar, you can twist a loop into the end of a piano wire; drill a hole the size of the wire into your base and sink the wire into this hole with a nail. The mobile is connected and planned exactly the same way as a hanging mobile.

Tabletop mobile. The suspension arm is a separate piece of wood which was doweled to the base after a hole was drilled into the bottom of the base and the suspension piece. Unusually red-toned pieces of wood were further color accented with the addition of tiny pastel shells and bits of red coral. Some additional pieces of the red-toned wood were placed at the base of the mobile, and one piece was tied to the protruding endpiece. (See color section.) Collection of Trudy and Sol Schwartz.

7 CARVING AND WHITTLING

The thrill which results from coaxing a design out of a solid block of wood has made whittling and carving popular pastimes as well as fine arts since primitive times. The professional wood sculptor usually carves only in selected hardwoods since soft woods tend toward too broad a grain and split and crack more easily. However, as more and more artists work seriously in wood, more and different theories about techniques and standards have evolved and many actually welcome the so-called weaknesses or "checks" in wood and incorporate it into their designs. Thus, found wood, ranging from soft boards to sturdy weathered stumps of cedar can be used to whittle and carve.

Small carvings require no tools other than an X-Acto knife (see Chapter 1 for illustrations of all the router blades available). Large, heavier logs will require heavier chisels and a mallet. If you have an electric tool such as a Dremel Moto Tool, you will find the use of the routing bit a fast, effortless, and most effective method of carving. Sometimes the wood you find requires just a bit of contouring, which can be done with rasps and sandpaper, or the electric Sando-Flex wheel illustrated in Chapter 2. This last is also helpful if you want a highly polished surface. Many wood carvers rub wax over the carved surface, leaving uncarved areas matte and unpolished.

BEGINNING WHITTLING PROJECTS

Many pieces of driftwood require only the most minimal carving to bring out certain high points or features. For your first effort at whittling, pick a variety of wood shapes. Turn each piece this way and that. A good piece will suggest two or three faces, either animal or human. Often all you will need to bring out the features you see will be some whittling away to bring a nose, a mouth, an eye, into prominence.

Study your wood for features you want to emphasize with your knife.

Turn the same piece another way to see if another, perhaps better, possibility suggests itself.

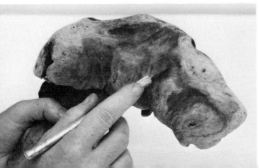

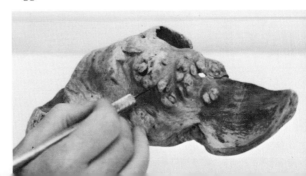

A group of driftwood pieces which have been whittled just enough to bring out features envisioned by artist Bill Gladstone.

RELIEF CARVING

Carving relief designs out of a plank of fairly soft wood is another easy project for the beginner. Here, it is best to plan your design by making a sketch directly on the wood. The area around the drawing is then routed out either with a knife or an electric routing tool until the design stands out clearly. The finished piece can be left as is or polished with deerhorn tip and wax. You can wax the relief area and leave the surrounding wood unpolished for contrast. Thinned paints or wood stains may be rubbed over the finished relief.

Draw a design directly onto the wood in pencil or India ink.

Whittle away around the drawing.

Relief by Joseph R. Hornings.

ELECTRIC TOOL CARVING

Electric router tools are excellent carving tools.

A naturally hollowed out sea horn with carved face.

CARVING ON A LARGE SCALE

When extending your carving endeavors to larger, heavier, and harder pieces of wood, you will find a good set of chisels and a mallet a good investment.

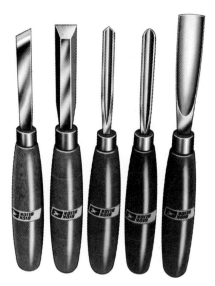

Basic tools for larger carvings. Photo courtesy Dick Blick.

A beautiful primitive figure carved from a log. The finished carving is stained with soft pastel pinks and blues. (See color section.) Collection of the authors.

Carved driftwood makes a handsome patio accent piece. Dell Mulkey, artist-photographer.

Carving from a found log and relief in weathered wood. Artist and photographer, Dell Mulkey.

Carvings made directly into railroad-tie and found logs. Bill Gladstone.

8 JEWELRY

The natural look in body adornment can be beautifully expressed with driftwood. The wood can be used as found or altered by means of carving to emphasize whorls and develop shapes. Flat pieces with well-textured surfaces can be sawed and cut to fit specific design concepts. The finished jewelry can be left natural or stained, varnished and/or waxed. Color and textural interest can also be added by combining driftwood with other materials such as ivory, coral, beads, and shells. In the following pages you will see just some of the infinite possibilities of driftwood jewelry making.

A supply of mechanical fittings known as jewelry findings will help you to make your jewelry wearable. Adjustable rings, closing catches, chains, jump rings are all available in inexpensive plated finishes either from your nearest jewelry supply store or by mail. (See Sources of Supplies.) A pair of pliers for opening and closing jump rings and metal nippers for cutting chain and wire are the only special tools you will need.

Pendants and Pins

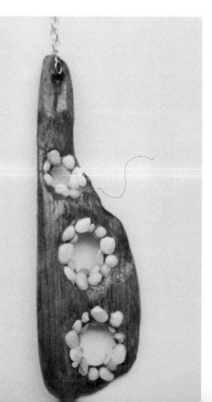

Each of these pendants is a natural formation. The little platform of the pendant at the left was sanded a bit flatter to accommodate the inlay of a sliver of ivory and a bit of red coral. Bits of red and pale pink coral were also glued to the grooves of the pendant at right. (See color section.)

The pin at left was made by routing out a section of the wood and inlaying the hollow area with crushed jingle shells. These delicate, almost translucent shells indigenous to the Florida coast can be crushed by hand, or in the blender. Mother-of-pearl inlay might be substituted but is much more expensive and these shells have an equally lovely iridescence. The pendant at right was a natural formation. The mother-of-pearl bead dangles freely from a piece of brass spool wire tied through the hole at the top. For an interesting effect which can be obtained with miniature driftwood formations and pearl beads see the Treasure Boxes illustrated in the color section.

Natural formation pendant, with two areas carved out to accommodate an inlay of ivory decorated with the woodburning tool. The ivory was recycled from tiles of an old Mah Jong set.

Shown here are some of the tiles from an ivory Mah Jong set. By cutting and slicing these pieces on a jigsaw both the etched and plain surfaces of the tiles can be used and the bits of undecorated ivory used for other types of inlaying, such as the woodburnt ivory inlay.

Holes were drilled and carved out, then tiny white shells were glued into the carved areas. A pale green finish was achieved by rubbing the pendant with a turquoise color pencil, and going over this with a bronze pencil. (See color section.)

Here is a closeup view showing how thinly the ivory tile can be sliced giving you lots of mileage out of a single piece. With ivory becoming more rare and expensive all the time, this is a good procedure with which to be familiar.

Here is a pair of ivory and driftwood earrings in the making. Two Mah Jong tiles have been sliced to preserve the original design, and sawed into a shape which conforms to that of the wood (also cut). The wood has been routed out so that the inlay fits in. This design could also be used for rings and pendants.

Rings and Earrings

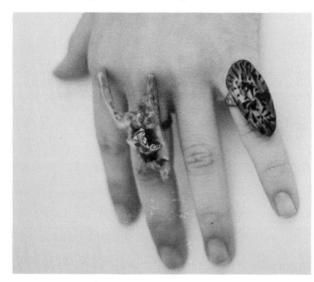

Both these rings are cemented to flat-topped adjustable rings. The pinky ring has a woodburnt design. The other ring is a natural formation, highly polished with a deerhorn tip and inlaid with a broken bit of an African glass bead.

Sue Holcomb searches through hundreds of little bits of curly driftwood to find pieces that match up. A pair can often be created by breaking long pieces in half.

Sawed Egyptian Collar Necklace

Flat beautifully grained driftwood sticks like this are easily found. Here a piece of wood is being marked for slicing.

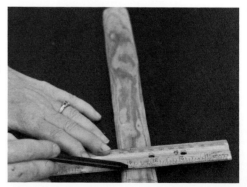

The beads which will make up the Egyptian collar necklace are sawed on an electric jigsaw. The sanding disc is in place to smooth the cut sides when needed.

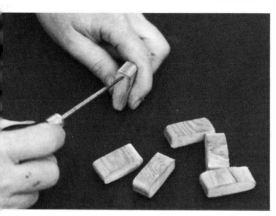

The beads are marked with an awl in preparation for drilling.

The finished Egyptian collar necklace. The brass spacers are washers from the hardware store. The necklace is strung on monofilament fishing line and closed with two jump rings and an adjustable hook.

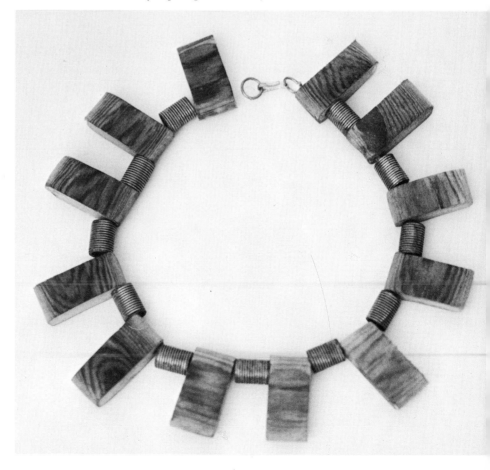

Indian Inspiration—A Driftwood and Bead Necklace

Indian-inspired design of beads strung onto cross-bars of driftwood. Two of the wood pieces are natural formations, one is cut and sawed. The beads are strung from top to bottom on 28-gauge spool wire.

The top portion of this necklace was found in this shape. The round wooden bead was cut on a jigsaw. The African glass beads contrast handsomely with the wood.

Little coils to prevent the wire from slipping through the holes of the first crossbar are made by winding wire around a toothpick.

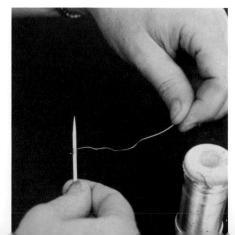

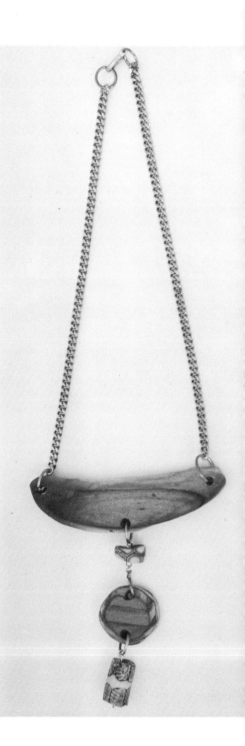

BRACELETS

Bracelets afford a fine opportunity to make use of lots of interesting little pieces of driftwood. The felt bracelet introduces a new type of material to combine with driftwood. Suede would work quite successfully also and would eliminate the first step of the demonstration.

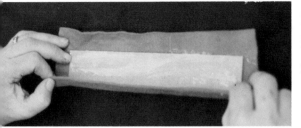

A piece of cardboard which will fit the wrist of the wearer when bent is covered with hot pink felt. It's best to glue the felt so that the edges meet at the center of the back. With a material such as suede this step is not necessary.

The driftwood design is glued to the bracelet before it is bent. Some white stones, tumbled to a translucent finish were incorporated into the bracelet. The bright pink of the felt shines through the stones.

The finished bracelet. Enlarged, it could be a dog collar . . . human or animal.

Polished abstract shapes combined into a handsome dangle bracelet. A finding known as a bellcap is cemented to the top of each piece of wood and hooked into the chain with a jump ring. Sue Holcomb. This bracelet could be enlarged and worn as a necklace.

9 FLOWERS AND DECORATIONS

For a long time driftwood as a craft was never mentioned without flower arrangements. Driftwood always played the supporting role and, as stated in the introduction, one of the purposes of this book is to take it out of the "prop art" category once and for all. Nevertheless, arrangements of all sorts are indeed very lovely when combined with driftwood, and in elevating the wood to star status, we don't mean to banish flower arrangements from the scene. In fact, we hope some of the ideas presented here to win some new converts to the art.

Just a bit of driftwood is needed as a base for a small arrangement of dried flowers. The flowers are attached to the base by sticking the cut stems into Styrofoam, and attaching the Styrofoam to the wood base with floral clay. If enough flowers are used the foam will be hidden. You can also tape a covering of florist's moss over the foam. (See the illustration for making a beach scene on sanded wood, Chapter 3, page 21).

SHELL FLOWERS AND DRIFTWOOD

The western coast of Florida, where Julia Hernberg lives, yields lots of interesting driftwood, but on a rather small scale. Since Julia is a miniaturist who specializes in making exquisite shell flower arrangements and shell-decorated eggs, she combines her arrangements of tiny shell flowers with small pieces of driftwood. The examples of her work which follow should provide some new ideas about floral decorations for even the most seasoned arrangers, and, at the risk of using a cliché, prove that good things can indeed come in small packages. All photos of Julia Hernberg's work by George Schupka.

Making a Floral "Gift from the Sea"

A bit of root about four inches long instantly suggested a laughing Sea Nymph which the artist envisioned as holding a "Gift from the Sea." The following demonstration photos show how a floral bouquet is made from tiny lilac shells, fitted into a natural shell container, and worked into the driftwood.

Tweezers and a pointed tool or pick are needed to work with the tiny shells used for the flowers. Here the pointer is used to place the pointed ends of the shells together on a very small drop of glue. The flower centers are made from tiny bits of crushed shell. They could be painted in. The stems are very fine brown wire.

Fine moss is placed into a sea urchin shell which will be the vase for the arrangement. You could glue a bit of Styrofoam into the vase instead of the moss.

Weeds or grasses are placed into the sea urchin shell.

Three tiny stones, the color of the root, are glued underneath to balance the arrangement and hold it in place. Another stone is glued into a strategic position at the back of the root to balance the whole thing.

Again using tweezers, the artist puts the shell flowers into the vase.

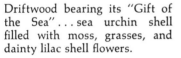

Driftwood bearing its "Gift of the Sea" ... sea urchin shell filled with moss, grasses, and dainty lilac shell flowers.

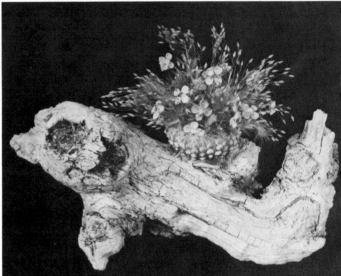

More Shell and Wood Arrangements

A piece of smoothly worn driftwood with a crevice just made to be a bird's nest. The nest is filled with fine green moss. The birds are made from cerithium (for the head), pointed venus (for the body) and squilla claws (for the wings and tails). Eyes and beaks are painted with acrylics, as well as wing tips and tails. A small stone is glued to the back to hold the arrangement upright.

A piece of delicately curved wood, often referred to as fairy driftwood, is mounted to a longer piece of wood to suggest a tree. A snake which is actually a dried piece of wood eyes two fascinating owls perched in the tree. The owls are made from alder cones and cerithium shells.

Fishbone and Sand Dollar Flowers in Driftwood

It was Julia Hernberg who introduced us to the "doves" hidden inside sand dollars. They were used as sea gulls in the sanded beach scene collage (Chapter 3) and here Julia paints them and uses them as flowers.

Moss and air fern seem to grow out of the holes in this driftwood. The flowers are made from the centers of a sand dollar.

The backbones of small fish can be equally lovely and useful. In the color illustration of the sanded beach collage, bleached blowfish bones were cut apart and used to suggest sea gulls. Here, we see them painted and mounted to resemble orchids.

Weather-beaten piece of silvery gray wood with pale green moss and tiny air plant inserted in the holes. The "orchids" are made from the backbone of small fish, painted to resemble the real flower, mounted on cloth-covered wire.

For another example of Julia's shell and driftwood art, see her real Ostrich Egg in the color section. It's mounted on driftwood and contains an interior scene of shell flowers on a miniature driftwood tree.

WEED HOLDER CONSTRUCTIONS

Driftwood assemblages often gain a special gentle grace with the addition of dried flowers and weeds, and many artists consciously add wood with weed-holding holes to their constructions.

Found wood box with driftwood and found wood. The dried flowers and pods are complemented by an airy bit of dried weed strung through a hole drilled through a dowel nailed to the side of the box as a graceful and creative afterthought. Artist Ahuvah Bebe Dushey. Photograph Stewart Schwartzberg.

Abstract Driftwood Flowers

The flowers themselves can actually *be* driftwood, to wit this exotic arrangement by artist Mary Prisco. Photo courtesy *Good Housekeeping.* Ernest Silva, photographer.

SEA HORNS AND DRIFTWOOD RINGS

Sea horns are considered true treasures by driftwood collectors. Actually, the sea horn is the joint where a limb is attached to a tree, or a branch attached to a limb. The long pointed shape is from the hardest wood of the tree which makes it a favorite with wood-carvers. (See carved sea horn, Chapter 7, page 00.) The horns are often found hollowed out and ready to be used as planters. They range in size from about six to ten inches. Driftwood suppliers will supply them to those unable to locate them on their own.

Driftwood rings are also lovely and lend themselves to many unique crafts ideas. They're somewhat easier to find than the sea horns, and, of course, certain solid shapes could be carved out until a hole is created.

Sea horn rings offer a challenge to egg decorators forever on the lookout for something new. Here, a tiny quail's egg is decoupaged with black and white designs and mounted inside a sea horn ring.

Sea horn with dried flowers.

Sea horn with dried pods, mounted into stiffened dried weeds which give a scrollwork effect. The dark browns of the weeds and some of the pods, blended with some paler browns into the very pale beige sea horn, makes for a striking monotone arrangement.

Dried leaves are glued around the sea horn ring to form a cartouche for a pair of adorable lovers made of tiny pebbles. The leaves at the front modestly hide the fact that the little stone people are not wearing any clothes.

For Christmas Giving and Decorating

A little driftwood boot would add a touch of whimsey to your Christmas tree. The one pictured here was found as you see it by Dee Weber. Bootlike formations are fairly common. The shapes can be emphasized with a bit of rasping.

Here's a great gift for a Christmas caroler—a whimsical choir made from small driftwood rings with small movable eyes added. Mount your choice on a block of wood and write your holiday greeting on the wood, or on a piece of chamois glued to the back. Artist Georgia Murphy.

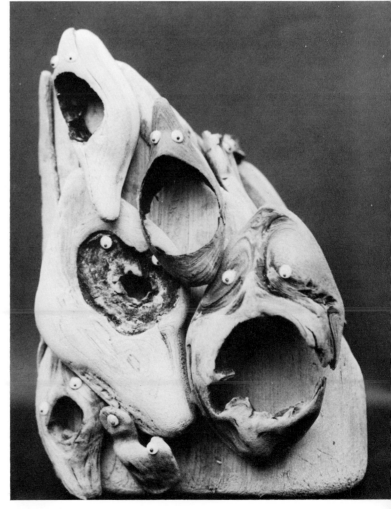

MAKING A WREATH

For a truly unique holiday wreath gather together lots of small pieces of driftwood. Fill in with pinecones, dried pods, pebbles, and bits of cork if you don't have enough for a full wreath. For the wreath base cut a twelve-inch circle from Masonite or a very heavy cardboard. You can cover your wreath base with paint, glue mixed with sand, dried moss, felt, burlap, or other scrap material. The wood is glued to the base with thick white glue such as Velverette. You can use small, flat, very ordinary sorts of pieces to fill out the base, then cover the top area with the showier, more outstanding pieces in your driftwood collection.

A wreath base with lots of wood pieces needed to make it a nice full design.

Finished wreath by Jerry Holcomb. Photo courtesy of the artist.

TURNING YOUR WREATH INTO A DECORATOR MIRROR

If you'd like your wreath to be a decorative year-round accessory, cut an extra circle. You might adjust the wreath size to a readily available round mirror to avoid having to go to the expense of having a glazier custom-cut a mirror to fit the wreath. Glue the mirror in between the extra backing wreath and the driftwood-covered wreath. Attach a hanging wire or hook to the back. The effect will be a round version of the mirrored cigar box assemblage shown in Chapter 4, page 00. Since the mirror is likely to be heavier than the wood, it is recommended that you use only Masonite or other wood, rather than cardboard.

10 KNOTTING AND WEAVING WITH DRIFTWOOD

Driftwood can be used in many unique and stimulating ways by the yarn and thread artist.

Weathered wood boards can be used to construct simple but very usable looms. The looms can be used as part of the design, rather than removing the weaving when it is finished. Pieces of wood can be woven in with the yarn to add exciting textural contrasts. Looms can even be found or constructed so that the driftwood itself becomes the warp or vertical section of the loom.

MAKING NOTCHED AND BOX LOOMS

A notched loom is a stronger, more durable version of the simple cardboard loom. V-shaped notches are cut at either end of the board. The vertical threads known as the warp of the loom are wound around the notches from top to bottom. The beginning of the thread is taped with masking tape to the back of the board and all the winding is done across the front. When the warp is complete the end strand is tied to the taped-down beginning. If the wood used for the loom has a rough surface in which the wool might get caught while weaving, sand it down before warping it.

Box looms work on the same principle as notched looms, with nails used to secure the warp. If you plan to keep your weaving on the loom, you can seal the wood with varnish or acrylic medium, and stain or paint it.

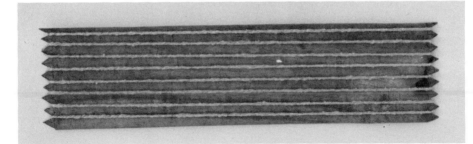

Notches on this simple board loom were cut out with a jigsaw. The warp thread is wound around each notch.

The warp is tied off across the back of the loom.

A box loom is constructed by nailing strips of wood to either end of the board. This will raise the warp up for easier weaving. Cut graph paper and hammer the nails into boxes marked off on the graph so your warp lines up evenly.

BASIC WEAVING PROCEDURE

The basic method is to weave yarn over and under the vertical warp threads. It is with the woof or horizontal weaving thread that you can really experiment with color and design. While the basic weave is to go over one and under one, you can create different patterns by going over three or four warp threads at a time, or under two or three. You don't always have to weave all the way across the loom. By weaving just partway across you can create open spaces. These could be filled in with different colors and textures of thread. You can weave in pieces of driftwood, as well as beads, stones, shells, and feathers.

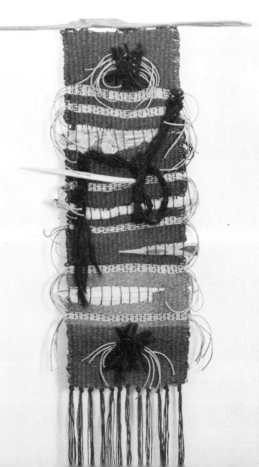

Pieces of driftwood woven into the design, with a large piece used as a crossbar. Mary Mendoza. (See color section.)

PERMANENT WOOD LOOM

You can make the wood loom a part of your design by cutting out a center weaving area with a jigsaw, leaving the frame as a decorative border for the weaving. Small nails should be hammered partway into the top and bottom of the loom. After the warp has been strung around the nails and the weaving completed, hammer the nails flush against the wood.

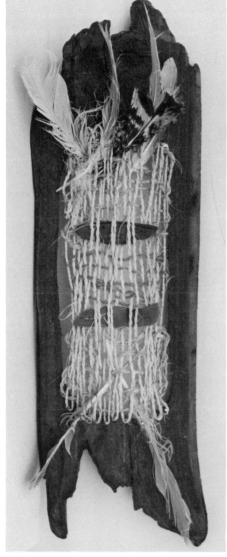

The shape of this wood seemed like a handsome frame for a simple, primitive weaving. Rough raffia cord in yellow and orange is used together with bits of wood and feathers.

Rear view of the weaving showing the cut made with the jigsaw.

Mary Mendoza constructed this handsome curved piece of driftwood into a loom which is an exciting and integral part of this stunning weaving. (See color section.)

WEAVING INTO WOOD BLOCKS

You can weave right into a solid piece of wood. Usually, a shape is chosen which suggests a certain type of weaving design. For example, the weaving in the demonstration which follows was done on a piece of wood with a natural protrusion which suggested a neck. This led to a rather whimsical woven construction with the weaving designed as a three-part cape and a head of a hen's egg, emptied out and stuffed with Instant Machie. The features were drawn in with India ink. While there are many pieces of wood shaped similarly to the "body" in the illustrated weaving, not all come complete with natural "necks," something which can, however, be easily remedied by adding a small piece of driftwood.

The warp for the main part of the cape to be woven is set up. The yarn is woven over the left section first to create a front opening.

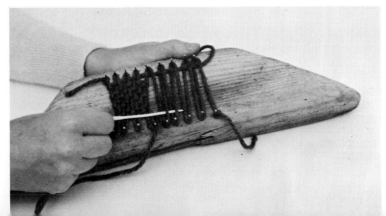

While the nails could be hammered into the finished weaving, they are re-
moved in this design and the loops are pulled, stretched out and glued down
with thick white glue.

When no natural "neck" exists, an additional piece can be glued or nailed
in place.

The finished egghead lady with her bright orange cape, a bit of a shell strung on
spool wire as a necklace, her head stuffed with Instant Machie.

WHEN THE WOOD ITSELF IS THE WARP

The wood for the spiderweb weaving shown below was found near the site where a house was being built. A tree had been cut down to make way for the building and this many-pronged branch was discovered among the cuttings. The branches looked like a spiderweb even before the weaving was added to carry through the spiderweb feeling. Two of the long ends were balanced into a flat base into which holes were drilled to accommodate the two resting points. The glued loom was allowed to dry thoroughly before the weaving was begun. Natural looms like this may not always be at your fingertips but you can make your own warp arrangements by drilling holes into a solid wooden base and gluing curved solid driftwood sticks into the holes. This in turn leads to more unusual weaving ideas, like the illustrated nylon weaving.

Moss green yarn is woven in and around the driftwood warp for a stunning spiderweb effect.

Wood warp created by drilling holes into a block of wood and gluing curved
driftwood sticks into a free-form loom. Holes are drilled into the wood warp
at various points so that the delicate pink nylon used as the weft can be
twisted through to create the design. The nylon is purposely pulled and
twisted to create additional rips.

The idea of weaving with old nylon stockings led to this sculptural weaving which
just had to be called Isadora.

MACRAME AND DRIFTWOOD

Mary Mendoza was a sculptor before she started to work with macramé. She has effected a happy marriage between the two crafts. She usually constructs her driftwood sculpture first, and then plans her macramé headdresses and costumes. The final result is a well-integrated work of art.

Two old ladies—or two companionable dogs? Take your choice. Mary Mendoza.

Feathers are woven into this Indian's striking macramé costume. Mary Mendoza.

A very regal "Judge Pelican" with flowing macramé robes and wig. Mary Mendoza.

CONSTRUCTION AND CROCHET

Everything and anything seems to be possible with driftwood. Ahuvah Bebe Dushey likes to do colorful little crochet patches to relax. As these crocheted pieces in bright pastel colors started to accumulate on her living room coffee table, she decided to work some of them into her wood constructions. These crocheted accents added color and delightful whimsical touches.

Wood construction with bits of colorful crochet. Ahuvah Bebe Dushey.

11 MISCELLANEOUS

SANDCASTING WITH DRIFTWOOD EMBEDMENTS

Since so much driftwood collecting is done at beaches, it seemed only natural to try to combine driftwood with another favorite beachtime craft, sandcasting. The excitement of working out a design right at the ocean's edge, then digging it out about a half an hour later, is something everyone should experience at least once.

Casting plaster is available at hardware stores or plumbing suppliers. Take along at least a five-pound bag. In addition to the plaster, you will need a large container for mixing. Plastic pails are best since they can be rinsed out. You can use the water from the ocean.

If you don't live near a beach or plan to visit one, you can do your sand-casting at home, using a sturdy box for your pouring. The box is torn away from the dried plaster.

In this demonstration project a large sun god was made. This is simple and very suitable for combining sandcasting with driftwood. Curved bits and pieces of driftwood make fine eyes and noses and mouths (don't use wood that is too light and thin or it will get buried in the plaster!). Unlike many other designs, the sun god eliminates the need to think in reverse which is usual with casting where the design is laid out face down.

Dig out your design near the water's edge so that the sand is wet. The border is indented with fingers. Wood features are laid loosely into place.

Plaster must be dribbled gently over the design so that the wood won't be weighted down and lost under the pressure of the plaster.

After about half an hour in the sun the plaster is set. Sand has been dug out all around the bottom of the design so that it can be lifted up easily.

The finished sun god can be left natural or painted with thinned acrylic paints.

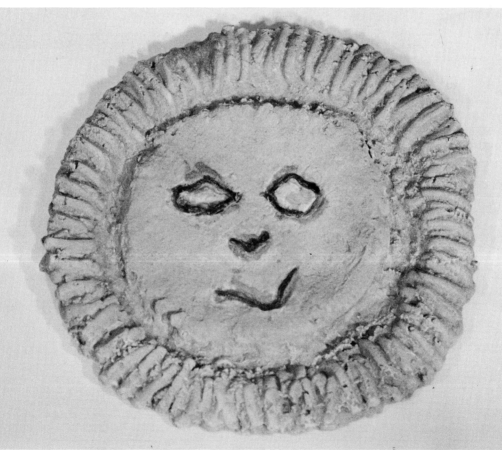

RUBBINGS FROM ETCHED WEATHERED WOOD

Most printmakers use very hard woods from which to make their woodcuts. However, by etching into driftwood with a hand tool, electric engraving tool, or even a woodburning pen, very handsome prints can be produced. When printing from odd-shaped pieces of found wood, the clearest prints seem to be produced when the paper or fabric to be printed is placed on top of the inked design, which is then rubbed through by hand or with a small rolling tool. Try printing your designs on different types of papers and fabrics. Construction paper, art tissue, and various rice papers produce lovely results. Fabrics such as burlap and cotton work very well. Your prints can be framed and hung or you could try making a scarf or a fabric to be sewn into a blouse with your own hand prints. If you use textile printing ink these will be permanent and waterproof.

To make a primitive face print, an appropriately shaped and very solid piece of driftwood was selected. The design is etched here with an electric engraving pencil.

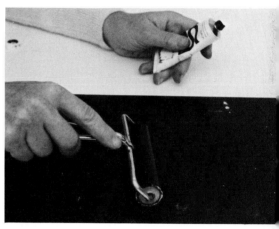

Printing ink (textile inks are recommended for fabrics especially) is rolled onto a piece of glass with a printing brayer.

The inked brayer is then rolled over the etched wood.

The paper to be printed is placed on top of the design and the impression is transferred by means of rubbing with a small roller.

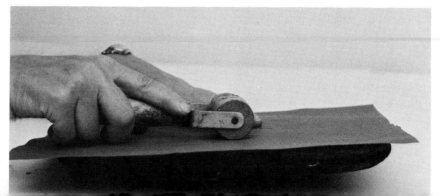

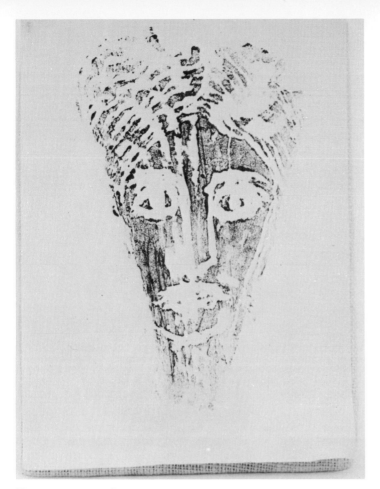

Print on construction paper.

Print on burlap.

86

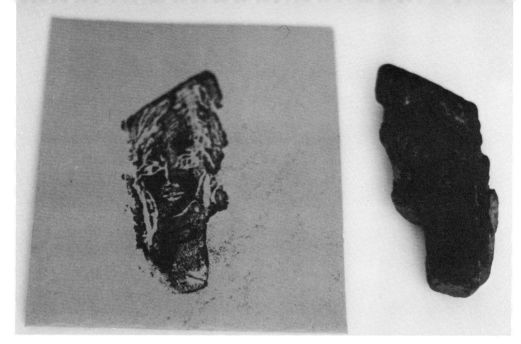

A small piece of driftwood was etched with a woodburning pencil and makes a handsome silhouettelike rubbing of a woman's head.

GREETING CARDS FROM RELIEF PRINT BLOCKS

You can create your holiday cards in an intensely personal way by making a simple raised-design printer. You will need a block of found wood larger than the design. Your design should be cut from a piece of wood about one-fourth to one-half inch thick. Words to combine with the designs can be made from plastic letters from children's print sets, mounted on wood.

A dove has been cut out of a piece of weathered board and mounted on a driftwood block.

Printing block of plastic letters glued to wood. Keep in mind the letters must be in reverse to come out correctly.

Doves and letters printed in white on blue construction paper.

For a wood-grained background texture, print the background with a well-grained block of wood. Then superimpose your raised design in a contrasting color. Here is black construction paper, turquoise wood grain, with white dove.

WEATHERED WOOD WALL CLOCKS

Almost any flat weathered board can be converted into a clock. To remain true to the basic material it's best not to think in terms of a perfectly rounded or square shape, else you might use any finished board just as well. Don't be put off by fragmentary edges and general unevenness of space. This will probably make your clock work in terms of artistic feeling and honesty. Stay away from anything too thick since you might have difficulty finding a clock with a shank that will pass through the center hole.

The clock shown here was made from an oddly shaped piece of wood with a gorgeous silvery patina. For the clock face, light-weight tooling metal, brass colored to match the handles of the clock, was cut out using a quarter as a template. The metal discs were adhered to the clock with cement, and a wood dowel was rubbed over the metal to bring out the grain of the wood beneath to the surface of the metal.

To add to the casual, seaside look, rope found at the beach was braided and nailed to the clock as a hanger.

Clock faces could also be created by woodburning or etching, painting, collage, or decoupage, to name just a few possibilities.

Weathered wood wall clock.

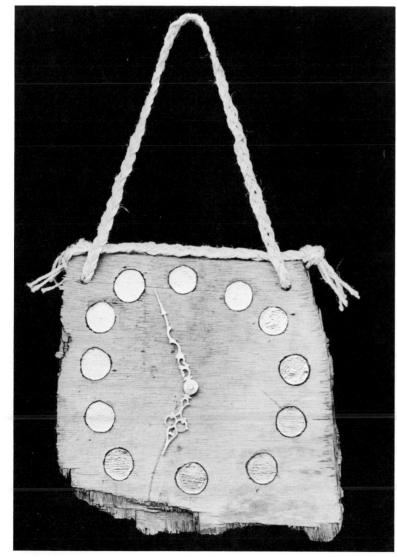

The New Wedding, Symbolized by a Driftwood Cross

On September 8, 1973, Shirley Hatfield married Joe Kitzman on the grounds of the groom's family ranch in Bandera, Texas. The young couple made their vows under a driftwood cross nailed together by two guests and hung into the cypress trees native to the area. Photo by J. O. Evans, Jr.

BIBLIOGRAPHY

ALEXANDER, MARTHANN. *15 Simple Ways to Weave.* Bloomington, Ill.: Mc-
Knight & McKnight, 1954 (Taplinger, N.Y.).

FRANKENFELD, HENRY. *Printmaking.* Audubon, N.J.: Hunt Manufacturing Co.,
1964.

HOLCOMB, JERRY. *Make It with Driftwood.* Brookings, Ore., 1971.

HUTTON, HELEN. *The Technique of Collage.* New York: Watson-Guptill Publications, 1968.

LYNCH, JOHN. *How to Make Collages.* New York: Viking Press, 1961.

MEILACH, DONA Z. *Contemporary Art with Wood.* New York, Crown Publishers, 1968.

———. *Macramé: Creative Design in Knotting.* New York: Crown Publishers,
1971.

MOSLEY, SPENCER; JOHNSON, PAULINE; KOENIG, HAZEL. *Crafts Design.* Belmont,
Calif.: Wadsworth Publishing Co., 1962.

PHILLIPS, MARY WALKER. *Step-by-Step Macramé.* New York: Golden Press,
1970.

PLATH, IONA. *Handweaving.* New York: Charles Scribner's Sons, 1964.

PRIOLO, JOAN. *Ideas for Collages.* New York: Sterling Publishing Co., 1972.

RASMUSSEN, HENRY, and GRANT, ART. *Sculpture from Junk.* New York: Rein-
hold Publishing Corp., 1967.

SCHAFFER, FLORENCE. *The ABC of Driftwood for Flower Arrangers.* New York:
Hearthside Press, 1951.

SOMMER, ELYSE. *Contemporary Costume Jewelry.* New York: Crown Publishers, 1974.

———. *Decoupage: Old and New.* New York: Watson-Guptill Publications,
1971.

———. *Designing with Cutouts.* New York: Lothrop, Lee & Shepard Co.,
1973.

SOUTAR, MERELLE. *The Driftwood Flower Arrangement Book.* New York: Funk
& Wagnalls Co., 1969.

STRIBLING, MARY LOU. *Art from Found Materials.* New York: Crown Publishers, 1970.

WEBBER, BERT. *Beachcombing for Driftwood, for Glass Floats, for Agates, for
Fun.* Medford, Ore.: Ye Galleon Press, 1973.

———. *Identifying and Working with Driftwood.* Medford, Ore.: Ye Galleon
Press (in process).

WILLIAMS, GUY R. *Making Mobiles.* New York: Emerson Books, Inc., 1969.

SOURCES OF SUPPLY

Acrylic Mediums and Paints

Hyplar
M. Grumbacher, Inc.
460 W. 34th St.
New York, N.Y. 10017

Liquitex
Permanent Pigments, Inc.
2700 Highland Avenue
Cincinnati, Ohio 45212

Adhesives

Cement
Bond Adhesives Company
120 Johnston Ave.
Jersey City, N.J. 07302

Epoxy
Devcon Corporation
Danvers, Mass. 01923

Miracle Adhesive Corporation
250 Pettit Ave.
Bellmore, L.I., N.Y. 11710

Sobo Quick and Velverette
Slomon Labs, Inc.
32–45 Hunters Point Avenue
New York, N.Y. 10010

Driftwood and Driftwood Accessories

Drift House
4337 Cottage Way
Sacramento, Calif. 95825
    Catalog: driftwood, deerhorn tips,
polish

Shells

Eggs for decorating and seashells
Julia Hernberg
1702 Cornwallis Parkway
Cape Coral, Fla. 33904
Send stamped self-addressed envelope
for list

Sea Shells and Supplies
Derby Lane Shell Center
10515 Gandy Blvd.
St. Petersburg, Fla. 33702

Florida Supply House
Box 847 Bradenton, Fla. 33505

Quail Eggs (small eggs)

Emma Birk
Route 1, Box 164
Frenchtown, N.J. 08825
Send stamped, self-addressed
envelope

Tools

Carving
Dick Blick
P.O. Box 1268
Galesburg, Ill. 61401

Sculpture House
38 E. 30th St.
New York, N.Y. 10016

Electric Drills and Saws
Black and Decker Mfg. Co.
Towson, Md. 21204

Dremel Mfg. Co.
Racine, Wisc. 53406

SandoFlex
Merit Abrasive Products, Inc.
201 W. Manville
Compton, Calif. 90224

X-Acto Co., Inc.
48–31 Van Dam
Long Island City, N.Y. 11101

Driftwood House
Box 2247 Highway 101 S.
Brookings-Harbor, Ore. 97415
   Catalog: driftwood, including sea horns, deerhorn tips, polish, pods, cones, etc.

Instant Machie

American Handicrafts (see phone book for address nearest you)

Dick Blick
P.O. Box 1268
Galesburg, Ill. 61401

Celluclay
Activa
44 Montgomery St.
San Francisco, Calif. 94104

Jewelry Findings

Jewelart, Inc.
P.O. Box 9
Tarzana, Calif. 91356

Sy Schweitzer & Co., Inc.
P.O. Box 431
East Greenwich, R.I. 02818

Sculptamold

American Handicrafts (see phone book for address nearest you)

INDEX